SUCCESSFUL GROWING

A Step-by-Step Guide
to Planting and Growing a Tree

John Klein

Absolute Author
Publishing House

SUCCESSFUL GROWING
Copyright © 2020 by John Klein
All rights reserved.

Publisher: Absolute Author Publishing House
Editor: Dr. Melissa Caudle
Cover Designer: John Klein

LIBRARY OF CONGRESS CATALOGUE-IN-PUBLICATION-DATA

Successful Growing/John Klein

    p. cm.

ISBN: 978-1-64953-105-6

    1.   Gardening 2. Agriculture 3. Planting Trees

PRINTED IN THE UNITED STATES OF AMERICA

Table of Contents

Preface

This guide provides high-quality information that people can easily follow to plant and grow a tree successfully. If you are interested in any of the following:

- Learning how to grow a tree.
- Saving money on energy, heating, and cooling costs.
- Making a memory with family and friends.
- Enjoyment for years to come.
- Saving the planet.
- Increasing knowledge to pass on.
- Gaining a green thumb.
- Enjoying the thrill of watching your tree grow strong and healthy.

The following content can then help you achieve these with thorough instructions and helpful tips on how to plant and grow a healthy tree of your own.

Chapter 1: Preparation

Assess the Size of the Area

When thinking of planting a tree, you should first consider what size of an area you have to work with to grow it. Your planting zone and the tree's expected size at maturity can limit the type of tree that you can plant in that spot. First, measure the dimensions of the area you want to plant the tree. For example, planting a Live Oak, which reaches over 100 feet in width at maturity, would not be appropriate in a 5x5 foot area. Indeed, you wouldn't want to have to cut that tree down in the future when it became too large for the space. Once you have determined the available area and types of trees that thrive in your growing zone, you must look at the next important factor in overall tree health, and that is the climate zone in which you reside.

Stay in the Zone

Another critical factor to consider for healthy tree success is knowing your USDA hardiness growing zone. Basically, this a number which is assigned to your area in the United States, (other countries will have one as well; check with your local Conservation office). Based on temperature and weather-related issues, this zone tells you which growing zone you currently live in. This is much-needed information, as it will determine what trees will grow, mainly based on temperature requirements. Also, different zones will have different climates, as some will have spring earlier, others later. Checking this is easy. A great website to use is one from the National Gardening Association listed below.

<u>USDA Hardiness Zone Finder - Garden.org</u>

Another great resource is located at the USDA Agriculture Research Service listed below.

<u>https://planthardiness.ars.usda.gov/PHZMWeb/</u>

Both of these websites are free to use, and they are easy to navigate; simply enter your zip code, and it'll calculate your planting zone. Knowing your zone is helpful in being successful when planting a tree; you wouldn't plant a palm tree in USDA hardiness zone 4b, which gets down to negative -25 degrees Fahrenheit! Take a few minutes, check your zone, and you'll save a lot of future headaches – trust me!

Light Availability Determines What Will and Will Not Grow

Next, you must determine the light available in the space. Is your intended planting area exposed to full Sun (defined by 8 or more hours of sunshine per day), is it exposed to partial Sun (defined as 4-6 hours), or is it in an area that receives limited sunlight/full shade (defined by less than 2 hours of light per day)? Certain tree species and varieties can perform well in one or two of these conditions but may not survive or perform well in an area where their particular light requirements are not met.

Always reference the plant's tag at the nursery for the sunlight requirement. If this is not provided on the tag, typically, a nursery associate can provide this information, or there are various reliable sources online. Caution: if you plant a tree that prefers full or partial sunlight in an area that receives complete shade, the tree will likely have limited growth (e.g., "stunting") and may eventually die.

Site Conditions are Everything

You'll need to figure out a general idea of what type of soil you have. Is your soil well-drained (a type of sandy loam), or is your soil compacted and water stays on top of it well after the rain passes (a type of clay loam)? Determining your soil type is key to your tree's health and longevity. Information regarding the tree's soil preference is located on the tree's tag when you buy it at a nursery, or available online.

To determine your site's soil type and conditions, you can perform a quick soil test. Items required:

- Shovel
- Watering hose/or canteen
- Water
- Tape measure or an equivalent measuring device to approximate length

Soil Test Procedure

1. Dig a 1x1 ft hole approximately 1 ft deep.
2. Fill the hole with water (do *not* overfill).
3. Allow the water to sit for at least 1 hour to saturate the soil.
4. Refill the hole with water, this time stopping when filled 2-3 inches from the top of the hole.
5. Allow the hole to drain for a minimum of 1 hour, preferably 2-3 hours, while continually measuring the amount of water drained out of the hole per hour in inches.

After 1-3 hours of hourly measurements, you can compare with standardized values to determine your soil conditions. If the water level in the hole drops:

- Less than 1/2 inch per hour: You have poorly drained soil and should be planting only wet-suited trees/species.
- 1/2 inch to 1 inch per hour: You have moderately well-drained soil, which is suitable for many species of trees, including wet-suited species.
- More than 1 inch per hour: You have well-drained soil, suitable for all species, including water sensitive trees that can handle being waterlogged.

Poor Drainage	Moderate Drainage	Good Drainage
Less than ½ inch water per hour	½ to 1-inch water per hour	More than 1-inch water per hour
Only Wet-suited tree's	Water-loving and wet-suited	All species of trees

Once you have identified the drainage level of your site, you should examine your soil type compared with the tree's preferences. Check whether the tree can grow in less fertile soils or if it requires rich soils. Most trees can usually tolerate a wide range of soil fertility, and the tree can amend their own soil via decaying leaves and branches if you allow these to act as a mulch for the tree.

If your soil is nutrient-deficient, you can enhance it with soil amendments such as manure, mulches, and fertilizer. However, I highly recommend planting a tree that will do well in your current soil conditions with no external work. This will save you a lot of time and energy.

Determining Which Tree to Plant

Now that you have a good idea of what you can grow at your site and have compared this with tree varieties of interest, you can confidently select an appropriate tree for your space. Remember to take your time and consider your options. This decision will stick with you and either fill you with regret or reward you for a lifetime.

However, don't take too long, because, as the saying goes, "The best time to plant a tree was twenty years ago, and the next best time is today." The sooner you plant, the sooner you will be rewarded with shade, beauty, and watching your tree grow.

Always consider the best and easiest times to plant are spring or early fall. Both seasons are easier on the tree but also easier to dig and less watering maintenance. These are also the time of year when the tree is relatively dormant. Thus, preventing a chance of shock when transplanting and allowing the tree and roots to acclimate.

It is best to plant your tree before or after the hottest time of the year, not during, so your tree can grow new roots and acclimate to the soil conditions. Your tree will be less likely to wilt or die if it becomes heat shocked. Please note that a tree is not necessarily dead if it loses its leaves in the growing season directly after being planted, it could just mean it is in severe shock. A little extra TLC and plenty of water and root growth fertilizer should get it sprouting new leaves before the end of the season. Early fall is another good time to plant due to your tree getting ready to go into dormancy; thus, it won't have quick stressors to ward off, such as the summer heat.

Dormancy is a deciduous process which includes most leafy trees, will lose their leaves and go into some type of hibernation. Conifers still go into dormancy as well, but most hold their needles instead of losing them. The tree is still living when it is dormant, and approximately half a tree's root growth happens during the dormant months, which are usually the colder months.

Chapter 2: Get Your Tree Home

Select Healthy Tree Stock from the Beginning

Depending on whether you buy your tree at a nursery or get it from a friend, you want to start with a tree that looks as healthy as possible, especially if you're paying for it! Some things to watch out for are as follows:

- Yellowing of leaves when they should be lush green.
- Holes bored through the tree trunk (caused by beetles or insects – is usually a bad sign that the tree is stressed).
- Look at the pot and the roots in it. Are they circling a lot, or are they wrapping around the tree? (also known as girdling). Granted, you can cut these roots off before finally positioning the tree in the hole, but

if you can avoid it from the get-go, you'll be a much happier person ☺

Always select a good, reputable nursery when purchasing trees, or even plants for that matter. The people who work there or the manager should be reasonably knowledgeable about the types of trees and species that grow in your region well. If not, buyer beware!

Pick a Good Starter Fertilizer

Purchasing a quality fertilizer will be vital in ensuring your tree gets off to a healthy start. You want to select a fertilizer that promotes root growth to accelerate a faster establishment. I recommend a natural-based fertilizer for the following reasons:

- Easier to use
- Doesn't burn the plant as chemicals can
- Feeds the soil, which in turn feeds the microorganisms, which will help your tree survive.
- It lasts longer; you'll only need to apply once a year.
- The cost difference is negligible and well worth any pennies more you'll pay upfront – it's always cheaper in the long run.

Remember, your planting for a generational statement, don't short your kids or their kids by selecting unhealthy, inferior products!

How to Read a Fertilizer

All fertilizers will have three numbers on them regardless if they are natural-based or chemically based that tell you the following amounts of each nutrient within the product.

N-P-K stands for:

- **N**itrogen (promotes leafy top growth essential for all plant growth),
- Phosphorous (Promotes root growth, you'll want a balanced or higher ratio of this to help with establishing your tree quicker!), and
- **K** stands for Potash (this will help in the overall vitality of your tree and help with getting trace minerals and nutrients to your tree, also aiding in the healthy trunk and bark growth).

Don't Forget Mulch

Remember to purchase mulch. When selecting a mulch, it's best to stay away from all those that say "Cologuard" or "keeps color for 12 months." All of these will have excessive dyes and even chemicals in them to be able to make that claim. Selecting a good quality bark mulch is preferred – if it's plain, that's the best! Bark mulch has more trace nutrients when it breaks down vs. sawdust; this is partly due to the bark mulch being derived from timber tree bark, which holds and stores the most nutrients, vs. the sawdust, which is the inside and core, which contains fewer minerals. Whenever possible – get bark mulch! You can utilize rotten alfalfa hay or rotten straw as well, or even pine needles, especially if the tree you're planting likes an acidic soil pH.

Weed Barrier

Having a weed barrier is more optional, though it will save you having to weed around your tree, especially early on. Weeds and unnecessary plants around your tree will compete for moisture and nutrients. If you choose, you would like the easier route, then select a good cloth fabric weed barrier to enable airflow to the roots and allow water to pass through.

Caution: Do not use plastic on the ground to suffocate weeds, as this will prevent water from getting through to your tree! Tree's need to have porous soil and the roots still breathe – much as our skin does.

Don't hinder this process if you can help it. If you choose to install this finish, backfill and applying fertilizer first. Once you do this, then use a small amount of mulch underneath this barrier; this helps add organic matter to the soil if low in organic material, then lay down the barrier and add the mulch on top to secure the barrier down to the ground. You may use stakes, though they're not necessary if you apply 2-3 inches of mulch around the perimeter of your tree.

Securing Your Tree Properly

Make sure you secure your tree correctly when taking it home and when you plant it if it's on the larger side as it may need support not to tip over. When securing your tree (if needed), always secure it to the lower half of the tree, preferably the tree's bottom foot.

This helps by forcing the tree to grow a proportional taper as the trunk extends up by getting wind and extra strain put to the bottom of the trunk (which naturally would occur).

This also helps the tree adapt to growing roots faster. If you place the support on the upper trunk, the tree will not get blown around as much, and the roots will not adapt to the growing conditions. The tree will become reliant on that to hold it up, not trying to support itself. Caution: Avoid twine as it could cut into the bark. If it's all you have, just be cognizant about how you use it. Remember to take all ties off your tree once it begins growing and supporting itself, especially if zip ties have been used, as these will surely girdle and kill your tree.

Avoid Damages

Between securing, loading, and bringing home your new tree, you will want to make sure the bark or any branches which are not going to be pruned aren't damaged in the process. This will put more strain on your tree, which is already going to go through some measure of transplant shock.

Water When Home if Dry or Climate Dictates

It's best to water your tree as soon as you get it home; this is especially true if it's a warm time of the year. If it's extra hot and sunny, place your tree in the shade for a few hours and let it replenish with water to the leaves and all parts of the tree before moving it to its permanent home. Think of your tree as a person and know that after a long trip with the wind, adding heat, it's like exercising for a person who requires hydration. Once you get to this point, you are getting closer to the reward of a lifetime of lower costs on heating, cooling, and leaving a great legacy for your children!

We are almost to the fun part where you can employ your task force of unlimited energy – the kids! ☺ (If, of course, you have them.)

Chapter 3: Planting Your Tree

Note: Always contact your county's underground dig hotline before digging any place in your yard to ensure you're not going to hit any existing underground pipes, lines, or anything that might be dangerous and or costly.

Dig the Hole for the Tree

Start by digging your hole outline; the final size should be 2X the pot's width and slightly shallower than the pot height. By doing this, you'll ensure that the tree roots can easily grow into the soil grade.

Also, you'll avoid the tree girdling itself by planting it too deeply. Girdling is where the tree wraps a root around the trunk, and over time, it grows and cuts off all nutrients and water, thus leading to mortality.

Place the Tree in the Hole

Remove the tree from the pot by tapping the pot's sides and lifting by the base of the trunk. If the tree is large or won't come out of the container, lay it on its side and repeat steps. If a tree is either too large or container won't come off due to roots growing out of the bottom, etc., just carefully use a utility knife or equivalent and cut down the entire length of the pot and into the bottom. The pot should peel off the tree's root zone easily.

Ensure the Roots are Good

Next, you want to make sure to scratch and pull away circling roots, pointing them down and out in the hole to get them started growing correctly. Cut any girdling roots, as discussed earlier, which are growing around the tree's trunk. It may seem harmful, though if you don't, it's worse for the tree long-term, and it will almost certainly die in time if not removed.

Face the Tree the Correct Way

Ensure your tree is facing the way you want it. The majority of limbs should be toward the sunnier side, same with the top. Whichever way it's already slightly leaning toward is the way the sunny side was facing before.

The sunny side is the direction the Sun is the brightest, in the Northern Hemisphere, that would be the southern direction. This side of the tree will have more limb growth, and the overall tree will grow slightly more this way than the other. Doing this will be easier for the tree to adapt due to replicating how it grew before at the nursery or its previous location.

Mix Fertilizer with Backfill Soil

Note: Avoid this step if using chemical fertilizer. If you're using natural fertilizer, mix roughly half the recommended fertilizer amount based on the manufacturer's recommendations for the tree's size with the backfill soil before backfilling. This will help put nutrients around tree roots, ensuring quicker absorption while feeding the soil at the same time. You do this with natural based fertilizer and not chemical due to naturally feeding the soil and your tree, which typically will not burn the roots as chemical fertilizer will. It is always best to avoid chemical fertilizer – you wouldn't digest chemicals or put them on your skin, so why would you give them to your tree?

Backfill Soil into the Hole with the Tree

While backfilling, make sure the tree's root zone is still slightly higher than the side of the hole (remember – plant high; it won't die ☺). Also, as your backfilling, make sure to fill the hole evenly to keep the tree's trunk straight and avoid having air pockets where there's an empty pocket with no soil. Once the backfilled soil is level with the soil line, lightly give it one last tamp.

Lastly, use the excess soil to form a berm of soil around the tree's outer root zone, ensuring you're not doing volcano mounding. Volcano mounding and or mulching is defined by piling soil or mulch up on the tree's trunk. Not only will this be very harmful to your tree by encouraging rot, but it will also encourage insect damage and will hold moisture against the trunk, thus keeping roots around the trunk and or forming a girdling environment for the tree. Making a berm for your tree will aid in watering, with fertilizer retention around the roots.

Once you're finished with this, get a drink, take a break, and be happy! You just finished the majority of the hard work! Congratulations, you're well on your way to completing your generational statement of planting a tree that your grandkids and generations after can enjoy! The next steps are critical in enabling your tree's short and long-term growth, thus resulting in a bigger and happier tree in a shorter amount of time.

Chapter 4: Fertilizing

If Using Naturally Derived Fertilizer

Back in Chapter 3, you will have already applied half your natural fertilizer. Now you'll finish. Carefully spread the rest of the fertilizer around the edge of the tree's drip line zone (also known as the root zone). This should be easy because you just planted the tree and should know exactly where that's at.

If you forgot, that's fine, as a general rule of thumb, you'll be safe on a newly planted tree to put it roughly one foot back from the trunk, 360 degrees around it.

The main reason you never put it on or by the trunk, no matter what fertilizer used, is the danger of burning the bark. Also, by placing it further out, you're encouraging the roots to grow out more to get to the rest of it. It's just like kids — you don't put the meal in front of them their whole life, or they get acclimated to that, thus expecting that much later in life. Instead, make them make their plate and get it! I call it strength building. ☺

If Using Chemically Derived Fertilizer

You will follow the same steps as the natural approach except for applying 100% of the fertilizer recommended on the label for the tree's size at the top of the soil, using the same method. With chemically derived fertilizer, you want to ensure to put plenty of distance from the tree's trunk, as it will almost certainly cause burn or damage to the tree trunk due to being much more aggressive and going into the soil very quickly.

There is no breakdown time to go into the soil like naturally derived fertilizer, which goes into the soil a little at first and then the rest over time. Chemically derived fertilizer is available to the plant as soon as it's applied, once watered in. Though it is preferable to use naturally derived fertilizer as it will still provide nutrients once watered, it will keep providing long after. You would have to keep applying chemical fertilizer types over again to get the same long-lasting result. Natural fertilizers rely on natural microbial activity that should be present in your soil for your tree's health anyway, to break it down and make it available for its absorption.

How Often to Apply and When?

For natural-based, you'll only need to apply once a year, typically (due to the nutrients breaking down over months), usually late winter just before spring starts is the best time, this will give it some time to work into the soil.

As for Chemically based, you'll apply a little later, typically once growth has started in the spring, as it's usually very quickly available to the tree. You'll apply this usually a few times during the growing season.

Follow the manufacturer's instructions, but as a rule of thumb, early spring as new growth starts, and then early Summer again with a lesser amount.

For the first year, I would recommend using less and stick with a higher phosphorous rated one not high in nitrogen. If you are wondering how to read this on the package, utilize chapter 2, where it's explained in detail.

Water

No matter which fertilizer you selected, you'll want to water it in thoroughly unless you have naturally occurring rain expected in your forecast that will do this for you.

Wash your Hands

Lastly, wash your hands well no matter if naturally based or chemically, you don't want that on your skin or in your body. Even the naturally derived types usually come from minerals mixed with animal byproducts.

Now let's move onto our next step not to forget!

Chapter 5: Watering

How Often and How Much to Water

Granted, you just finished watering because you fertilized, but you'll still need to remember to water your tree. As a rule of thumb, you'll need to supply water at least every two weeks throughout the growing season if not achieved by the weather. Though if extremely warm, you may end up watering every 3 to 4 days, even with mulching your soil around the tree well. Apply approximately 1-5 gallons for small trees under 1-inch caliper on the trunk or 5-15 gallons for bigger trees. You'll water enough to get the top several inches of soil around the tree thoroughly wet, not waterlogged.

Best Way to Water for You and the Tree:

The best and easiest way to water your tree effectively is to get either a drip irrigation system set up or put a hose to your tree. Turn it on, so it's just barely trickling out, perhaps maybe a gallon every 10 minutes, though approximating is fine. Then leave it for about an hour, come back, move it to the other side of the root zone, and leave it for another hour or so.

Check to ensure your soil around the tree is well-watered by inserting your finger into the soil/mulch a few inches. Watering this way is the best for you and the tree. This gives the tree more time to absorb the water more effectively over a much longer period, rather than dousing it in a few minutes or less. It's like a person – if you give two people each a gallon of water to drink, but one has 8 hours, the other only has 1 hour, who is better off throughout the day? This will be one of your most important things to stay on top of for at least the first two growing seasons, though the size of trees and weather will dictate.

For small trees, they should be fully established in about 1-2 years. For larger trees, they will take anywhere from 2-5 years to establish fully. Each year should require less extra watering, though. Once fully established, you can sit back and reap the rewards of all your hard work! The next chapter is crucial to achieving good form and a sound structure for your tree from the start!

Chapter 6: Pruning (if needed)

What Look or Goal are You Trying to Achieve?

Whenever starting a project, the first and foremost thing you do is consider your end goal. This question could be a short answer or a loaded one that needs thorough answering. Suppose your tree is deciduous, and you're wanting only shade from it. In that case, it's in your best interest to create a strong structure from the beginning of an upright structure with only one central trunk, turning into a wide branched canopy about 10 ft off the ground.

Suppose you are looking for a windbreak from a conifer. In that case, you might want to consider pruning to one central leader and keeping as many horizontal limbs as possible for maximum effect. If you're growing a fruit tree, your goal will be to prune and top your tree early, say at 3 feet, or wherever you would like it to start forming horizontal branches. The distance from the ground in which you would like to pick fruit will dictate this. You'll keep pruning as it grows year after year to achieve a wide, bush-like form. This will end up being the strongest for fruit production and will usually almost always yield the most fruit. Your goal will dictate this, with a few exceptions to look at.

What Time of Year is Best to Prune?

Timing is critical, unless, of course, a branch has broken, then no matter what time of year, you'll need to remove it. For all other cases, the best time to prune most trees is actually in mid-winter; this is due to the tree being in full dormancy, and the sap production will be at its slowest, which will help conserve its vital resources. Think of it as a wound for a human – if you're bleeding, it's easier to control and fix the problem when your heart rate is slower, and you don't lose all your blood rapidly. It's better if it's slower due to bleeding out less and leaving less room for infections. Treat your tree similarly.

Also, insects will not be an issue at this time. The thick sap that naturally attracts beetles and other bugs that would love to burrow into your tree will be dead or hibernating, giving your tree a free window of time to not be producing that attractant anymore by the time spring comes.

Why You Should Prune some Unneeded Branches

Pruning after planting a tree is a great thing to do for it. Due to transplant shock, it could be going through a severe shock of not having enough root mass laid down for the tree's top. To ensure this doesn't happen, it's beneficial to take some of the strain off the tree by cutting low or unwanted limbs that will end up getting pruned anyway within a year or two.

Warning: Don't prune too much, any more than ¼ of the tree is a dramatic prune and will be too much, causing the tree to go into further shock due to not having enough limbs and leaves for photosynthesis, which is the process where your tree feeds itself. This is done when it takes in Carbon-dioxide and produces Oxygen in return. This CO_2 feeds your tree. Remember – everything in moderation.

Type of Tree Will Dictate Structure and Form

If you're working with a conifer type of tree, you will not want to top it due to many conifers when topped, never grow back the same, or don't heal properly.

On the other hand, most deciduous trees can take being topped if appropriately done and still thrive. Remember, the best structure, unless desired for fruit or a bush, for any tree is usually straight up with one central trunk. This form is usually the strongest structure for most, if not all, trees.

How Much You Can Prune and Why

As stated earlier, when you prune a tree, it takes away the potential for it to photosynthesis and creates less energy and food for the whole tree, including the roots. The roots and bark are where much of the tree's nutrients, minerals, and foods are stored. The leaves merely act as a food producer, generating food for the tree by absorbing CO_2 out of the air and producing Oxygen for our great planet.

A good rule of thumb to follow is never to prune more than 25% of a tree in any given year. If you get a big tree, I wouldn't prune for multiple years after that. When over-pruning, you run the risk of sending the tree into shock, and one of two things could happen, it could send a lot of new branches everywhere, even where you didn't want them, and these new branches will be much weaker due to rapid growth rings and poorer form than the original.

On the other hand, it could go into dieback, meaning it would die back in the roots due to starvation of food, thus dying back on the top of the tree. This is a less likely scenario, though there is a higher chance with new, weak plantings, and/or especially old trees.

How to Prune for the Quickest and Best Tree Healing

When pruning, you want to ensure you're pruning the correct spot of the branch collar. This spot is typically easy to see – look at it from the side, and you'll notice it if it's difficult to spot at first.

The branch collar is where the branch comes off the main trunk and starts to extend out; it is almost always wider, then it tapers to the branch size. Where it stops tapering, just before that is the branch collar, usually, it's an inch or two on big trees, and on small trees, it's a very small size.

Proper Pruning Principles

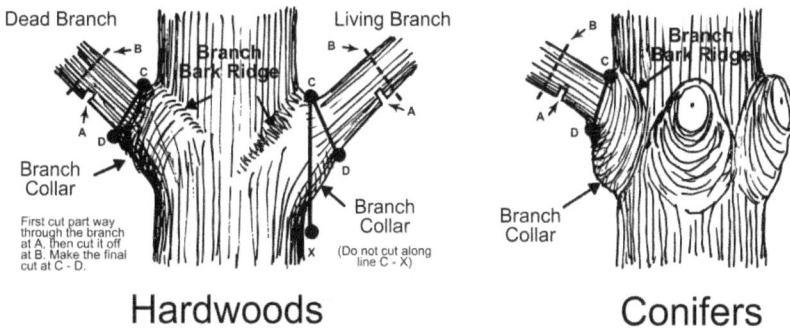

Dead Branch — Living Branch

Branch Bark Ridge

Branch Collar

First cut part way through the branch at A, then cut it off at B. Make the final cut at C - D.

Branch Collar
(Do not cut along line C - X)

Branch Collar

Branch Bark Ridge

Branch Collar

Hardwoods **Conifers**

Arbor Day Foundation

Source: Arbor Day Foundation

When pruning, it's best to make at least two cuts, one farther back, taking off most of the weight of the limb being cut, and another finishing cut closer to the tree's trunk where it should be cut for proper healing. Tip: If you're doing large limbs, it will be helpful to cut multiple cuts to avoid your saw pinching when cutting, also you'll negate the risk that the limb splits off when cutting, peeling back into the trunk.

Pruning here will allow the tree to heal, where it would otherwise rot from being opened too long, especially on large trees. You'll notice if done correctly, the tree will heal very quickly. If not done correctly, it can leave lasting, damaging effects.

If pruned too close to the tree, especially on large trees, you will get rot that could proceed back into the tree's trunk. If pruned too far away, leaving a branch or nub, you won't get the healing effect. The tree will try to heal around it by cutting off nutrients and water to the limb by basically girdling the limb. This method is not a healthy way to leave your new tree. Be cognizant always – it will pay off for you and your tree!

Always Use a Clean Saw or Pruners

This is an area that is quite neglected for most homeowners and even professionals. If you have cut another tree recently and you use it on your new tree without washing it off with a scrubber and/or soap, you could potentially be bringing a new disease or fungus to your new tree. This is especially problematic if you're pruning the same species, and one has a fungus or disease – you'll be transferring it to your new tree! Not a good idea!

Always remember that you are the best defense of protection against stopping this. Never allow this to happen; carelessness turns into problems quickly, and sometimes devastating ones! You've worked too hard at this point to short yourself on something that takes less than a minute to do.

Chapter 7: Mulching Your Tree; It's Benefits

Benefits of Mulch

Mulch offers many benefits to your tree and the environment as a whole. Did you know that mulch conserves water, leading to less frequent watering, saving you time and money? Also, mulch breaks down over time, adding to the soil's organic matter, which builds your soil up, adding to your topsoil layer over time.

Mulch mimics a tree's natural environment of a forest system which has leaves, dead limbs, etc. naturally decaying under the canopies of the trees. In turn, this helps to increase mycorrhizal in the soil, a naturally symbiotic relationship that all plants and trees need to survive.

Mycorrhizal is a fungus, a type of mushroom that lives in the tree's roots, and feeds off the sugar that the tree sends to its roots; the tree cannot utilize this sugar it would otherwise be wasted. In return, the mycorrhizae extend the tree's roots into the soil with their filaments and increase a tree's root system and drought resistance more than ten-fold.

In city soils or any for that matter that is severely compacted or high in pesticides or herbicides, the mycorrhizae are often not present or dead due to these conditions, leaving a tree to fend for itself and be severely weaker and unhealthy. Nature knows best – remember that!

Why You Should Mulch

Besides the benefits mentioned above, a good reason is to make your life easier. Mulch suppresses weed growth, and if applied correctly with a weed barrier, will stop all weeds from growing. Mulch keeps the soil moist longer, retaining water longer, and also keeps the soil cooler, thus helping alleviate tree roots from frying under the surface in the hot Sun. Mulch adds good minerals to the soil and makes for a healthy happy tree!

What Type of Mulch?

The type of mulch you use will strongly be dictated by the following:

1) Your area and what's available,
2) What kind of look you are trying to obtain, if any,

3) Price, and
4) Benefit you're trying to achieve.

Bark derived mulch usually always has the best mineral and nutrient content compared with sawdust, which comes from the inner trunk of trees. Both are generally slightly acidic in pH, which helps any tree which likes a slightly acidic pH.

Sawdust usually is a lower pH as well. Other types of mulch that usually aren't as readily available include pine straw, which is highly acidic or compost via animal or plant matter; this adds lots of good nutrients, though it's less utilized due to price and look. Also, if you can get it – rotten straw or alfalfa hay is sometimes the best mulch if applied with a layer of bark mulch as a top dressing (mainly to keep the look of aesthetics).

When your mulch is adequately decayed before applying, it won't suck any nitrogen out of the soil, which almost all fresh mulches will do during their decaying process. These have high nutrient content, especially the alfalfa. Just be careful with all mulches, especially if using fresh new sawdust; it will deplete your soil from some nitrogen, so to offset that, add a little more nitrogen to the soil via manure or a naturally high nitrogen fertilizer such as blood meal.

The type of mulch you select is entirely up to your preferences, though I prefer bark mulch to keep it simple, and it looks good in almost all situations.

What to Avoid

Things to avoid for mulches are high cypress quantities due to its suppressing growth attributes that prohibit many species of plants and trees from growing. It has a natural chemical compound in it. Also, walnut is similar in that it excludes a lot of species from growing around it. Don't use these leaves or mulches around your tree. When purchasing mulches, such as bark mulch, stay clear of anything that says color-guard or guaranteed color for x number of months.

This simply means that the company has added a dye or chemical to it, and thus is not beneficial to your soil, your tree, or any of the organisms that live in the soil and help your tree survive.

How Often to Re-apply?

Your soil type, the quantity of microbial activity, moisture content, and rainfall of your area will all dictate how quickly your mulch breaks down, and turns into rich soil, and "disappears," transforming into great new soil! As a rule of thumb, you'll typically renew your mulch once a year in the spring or fall. Usually, re-applying won't take as much mulch as your first application due to already having a good mulch layer on the soil. All you're doing is renewing what has decayed.

How much Mulch to Apply, and How to Properly Mulch

As far as mulching is concerned, you'll want to mulch at least 2-3 inches spread evenly across the soil 360 degrees around your tree, not allowing it to pile up on the trunk. Avoid placing any more than 4 inches on the soil, as this is unnecessary and will suffocate the tree roots rather than helping them – plus cost you more money!

You'll want to place mulch for small trees at least a foot out, 360 degrees around. It is beneficial for larger trees to spread over an area of 4-6 feet out from the trunk. The bigger your tree gets, the better it is to increase the mulch line, as the roots of a typical tree extend 2-3 times the spread of the canopy – the horizontal branches.

If coniferous (needlelike), the tree's height plus or minus a little will be the root spread.

Caution: Never pile mulch up on the tree's trunk; keep it at least a few inches from the trunk, as piled up mulch will favor rot, decay, and insect problems. Always remember – everything in moderation. Happy Mulching!

Chapter 8: Reoccurring Maintenance

Watering

Don't skip out on watering your newly planted tree! It will need frequent watering during the active growing season, mainly the Summer, especially through spells of drought and dry times.

You should be checking your tree at least once a week, twice a week during dry, hot times, ensuring sufficient water by using the soil finger method, testing if the soil is still fairly moist or not.

Fertilizing

Late winter or early spring, you should feed your tree with a healthy natural fertilizer, such as an all-purpose, blood meal, or an acid-loving mix, depending on tree type and preferences.

Ensuring your tree is fed will help to improve lush, healthy growth and make it less susceptible to insect predation.

Mulching

Renewing your mulch annually once a year will ensure your tree's root system stays happy and healthy. It will also ensure healthy microbial activity exists, thus helping your tree grow the root system becoming massive!

Pruning

Ensure your tree stays free of any broken or dying limbs, which is essential in keeping your tree's hygiene healthy. As your tree puts on growth, you may consider limbing your tree up, thus cutting low limbs off till you get the desired height. You must do this slowly on an annual basis to make sure you don't take away from the carbon (food) producing limbs that feed your tree. Just remember that pruning should be done in the mid-winter months to ensure all insect predation is at its lowest, also preventing your tree from going into shock.

Take Pictures (Optional)

You've worked this hard to accomplish making a generational statement, something your kids and possibly even their kids can enjoy, depending on tree variety, of course. Now, indulge in the experience!

As your tree grows into an adolescent, a teenager, and adulthood, take pictures with it. This will allow you to have a record of the progression of it, as well as to allow family members and friends to see in the future how something so small turned into something truly amazing!

Have fun and enjoy your fruits or shade!

About the Author

I grew up on a small farm outside McMinnville, Oregon, located in the Willamette Valley. I learned a lot about myself and how to grow plants successfully. I learned how to grow many different fruit trees, shade trees, windbreak trees, and traditional and herb gardens at a very young age. I had many encounters with Mother Nature in the countless crops I grew. Some years were better than others, but by sticking to time-tested methods of propagating plants, I learned better ways to negate most horticulture risks. Hands-on farming was not the only way I learned. I took instructional classes on horticulture, forestry, and outdoor management. When I couldn't answer, I would do countless hours of research online from various sources and then implement them into the landscape to determine what worked and what didn't. Today, I bring to you the very best of my knowledge and insight into a wide array of common plant-related issues. I believe that the best way to grow anything successfully is by sticking with what Mother Nature intended. Deviation from this will typically lead to struggles. By reading this guide, I hope you can avoid pitfalls when planting and growing your tree.

Happy growing friends!
-John Klein

INDEX

www.ingramcontent.com/pod-product-compliance
Lightning Source LLC
Chambersburg PA
CBHW071748020426
42331CB00008B/2227